THE REALLY BEASTLY JOKE BOOK

Aargh! For ghostly giggles and spaceships
full to bursting with hilarious jokes from
outer space, don't miss . . .

THE HAUNTED JOKE BOOK
THE ALIEN JOKE BOOK

also by John Byrne,
published by Corgi Books

▲▼▲▼▲▼▲▼▲▼▲▼▲▼▲▼▲▼▲▼▲▼▲▼

JOHN BYRNE

THE REALLY BEASTLY JOKE BOOK

▲▼▲▼▲▼▲▼▲▼▲▼▲▼▲▼▲▼▲▼▲▼▲

▲▼▲▼▲▼▲▼▲▼▲▼▲▼▲▼▲▼▲▼▲▼▲▼▲▼

For Travis Prosper

THE REALLY BEASTLY JOKE BOOK
A CORGI BOOK : 0 552 54624 0

First publication in Great Britain

PRINTING HISTORY
Corgi edition published 1998

3 5 7 9 10 8 6 4 2

Copyright © 1998 by John Byrne

The right of John Byrne to be identified as the author of this
work has been asserted in accordance with the Copyright,
Designs and Patents Act 1988

Set in 12/15pt Tiffany by
Phoenix Typesetting, Ilkley, West Yorkshire

Corgi Books are published by Transworld Publishers Ltd,
61–63 Uxbridge Road, London W5 5SA,
in Australia by Transworld Publishers,
c/o Random House Australia Pty Ltd,
20 Alfred Street, Milsons Point, NSW 2061,
in New Zealand by Transworld Publishers,
c/o Random House New Zealand,
18 Poland Road, Glenfield, Auckland,
and in South Africa by Transworld Publishers,
c/o Random House (Pty) Ltd,
Endulini, 5a Jubilee Road, Parktown 2193.

Made and printed in Great Britain by
Cox & Wyman Ltd, Reading, Berkshire.

▲▼▲▼▲▼▲▼▲▼▲▼▲▼▲▼▲▼▲▼▲▼▲▼▲▼

FOREWORD

W– what's that m-moving in the undergrowth? Oh – it's just you, the r-readers. Yes, it's m-me Quentin Quiver again and I'm in my very favourite place . . . as far away from modern civilization as I can possibly get.

It hasn't been easy getting out here – even with my map and compass I got lost three times and thought I'd never be heard of again. And that was just on the way out of my bedroom! But at last I've made it to this peaceful, green spot where there's nobody else but me and Mother Nature.

So if you too are looking for something a bit different to those h-horrible rude joke books which sadly seem to be so p-popular with young people nowadays, you've come to the right place.

Because the book you're holding in your hands is going to be called *Quentin Quiver's Book of Gentle Jokes and Flowery Fun* and I'm about to start working on it right now. I see you're not laughing very much yet – never mind. Because the whole point of me coming out here is so I can work on it in complete peace and quiet, with nothing to disturb me but the gentle whisper of the wind in the trees, the soft ripple of a jungle stream and of course the savage growl of that huge man-eating tiger . . .

    Hang on – did somebody say t-tiger?

DON'T WORRY QUENTIN – IT'S NOT A TIGER..

ARRGH!

NO – IT'S LOTS OF TIGERS – NOT TO MENTION LIONS, ELEPHANTS AND RHINOS TOO!!

JUST TURN THE PAGE AND SEE WHAT HAPPENS WHEN YOU TRY TO MONKEY WITH OUR JOKE BOOK!

GET READY FOR JOKES THAT ARE FUNNIER THAN HUMANLY POSSIBLE!

Chapter One

WHY DID QUENTIN QUIVER CROSS THE JUNGLE?

BECAUSE THE GIANT SNAKE THOUGHT HE'D TASTE NICER THAN THE CHICKEN!

What is a giraffe's favourite fruit?
Neck-tarine.

Why did the ape lie down in the sun?
He wanted to get an orangu-tan.

What do you sing to a python on its birthday?
'For squeeze a jolly good fellow . . .'

Why should you never believe anything a koala tells you?
Because he might be a bear-faced liar.

Where do you take sick kangaroos?
To the Animal Hop-pital.

What's big and grey and always running
a temperature?
An illephant.

What do you say to a hyena on its
birthday?
Many ha-ha-ha-ha-ha-happy returns.

Why did the skunk buy a lottery ticket?
He wanted to be stinking rich.

Why didn't the worms go into Noah's
Ark in pairs?
Because they went in apples.

Guide: Quentin, I've got some good news and some bad news. The good news is there are no huge, savage tigers in this jungle.

Quentin: So what's the bad news?

Guide: They moved out to escape the huge, savage lions.

What do you get if you cross a parrot with a tiger?

I don't know – but when it talks you'd better listen.

What does the mummy cobra say to the
baby cobra when it's raining?
'Don't forget to put up your hood.'

At what time is a wild animal most
likely to sneak inside your tent?
Whenever the flap's open.

Why did the mummy cobra have to stay
at home with her kids?
She couldn't find a baby-spitter.

What did the camel say after three
weeks in the desert?
'Long time, no sea.'

What school subject do snakes like best?
Hiss-tory.

What do you get if you cross a skunk and an angel?
Something that stinks to high heaven.

How do you know if a seal is hiding up a tree?
Listen to the bark.

I DIDN'T EXPECT TO FIND A SEAL IN THE JUNGLE...

I KNOW...BUT I HEARD YOU WERE A FISH OUT OF WATER...

What was wrong with the sick chicken?
It had people pox.

Why didn't the centipede enjoy practical jokes?
It didn't like anyone pulling its leg, leg, leg, leg, leg, leg, leg, leg . . .

What's worse than a centipede with a wooden leg?
A giraffe with a sore throat.

What's worse than a giraffe with a sore throat?
An eagle that's afraid of heights.

What's worse than an eagle that's afraid of heights?
An elephant with a blocked nose.

What's worse than an elephant with a blocked nose?
A tiger with a tiny headache.
Hang on – a tiny headache's not bad compared to all those other things . . .
I know – but are YOU going to tell that to the tiger?

What did the pig do when the wolf bit his bottom?
He rubbed on some oinkment.

Why do mice need regular oiling?
To stop them from squeaking.

What do elephants say when their calves misbehave?
'Tusk, tusk!'

What do you get if you cross a bee with a cow?
A humburger.

Why did the leopards have exactly the same spots?
Because one of them was a copy-cat.

How do you hire a camel?
Put a brick under each of its legs.

What's the world's biggest ant?
A gi-ant.

How do you catch a squirrel?
Climb up a tree and act like a nut.

How do skunks fly?
In their smelly-copters.

Why was the elephant's trunk only eleven inches long?
Because if it was twelve inches long it would be a foot.

Which animal is best at giving advice?
The skunk – because it always makes a lot of scents.

SO, QUENTIN – HOW ARE YOU ENJOYING THE GREAT OUTDOORS?

'ORRIBLE NIFF

≥COUGH!≤ IT'S G-CERTAINLY TAKING MY ≥CHOKE!≤ BREATH AWAY...

What do you get if you cross a telephone with a crocodile?
Snappy answers.

Which side of a tiger has the most fur?
The outside.

Why do mosquitoes hum?
Because they have forgotten the words.

Why couldn't the animals on the Ark
play cards?
*Because two elephants were sitting on the
deck.*

Why didn't the elephants go for a swim?
They'd forgotten to bring their trunks.

Where do polar bears dance?
At a snowball.

What did one goat say to the other goat?
'I wish you'd stop butting in.'

What do you call a musical spider?
A guitar-antula.

What's big and grey and never gets to dance?
Cinderelephant.

Chapter Two

HOW MANY BATS DOES IT TAKE TO CHANGE A LIGHT BULB?

NONE...IT'S MORE FUN TO CHASE QUENTIN IN THE DARK!!

HELP! I CAN'T SAY I'M 'DE-LIGHTED' WITH THE WAY THINGS ARE GOING!

What's sweet and sugary and swings
through the jungle?
A meringue-utan.

What do you call a tiger on the beach?
Sandy Claws.

Where would you find a tortoise with no
legs?
Wherever you left it.

What do you get if you sit under a cow?
A pat on the head.

Why did the three wild pigs leave
home?
Because their parents were terrible boars.

Why did the elephants use the skunk as
a football?
They wanted to kick up a stink.

Why did Quentin Quiver put insect spray inside his shoes?
Because he had no mosqui-toes.

Did you hear the joke about the bald porcupine?
Yes – but there's really no point to it.

▲▽▲▽▲▽▲▽▲▽▲▽▲▽▲▽▲▽▲▽▲▽▲▽▲▽

Why do the hyenas like playing Monopoly?
Because they're game for a laugh.

'Waiter, there's a fly in my soup!'
What do you expect for a pound, sir – an elephant?'

'Doctor, Doctor, I keep thinking I'm a python.'
'I find that rather hard to swallow.'

What do you get if you cross a jeep with a dog?
A Land Rover.

Why did the kangaroo stop jumping?
Because it was out of bounds.

Why is Quentin Quiver like the jungle?
They're both very green and incredibly thick.

How do skunks wrap their Christmas presents?
With rolls of smell-o-tape.

What do you get if you cross a snake with a snowman?
Frostbite.

What do polar bears keep in their wallets?
Ice lolly.

First Wolf: Where does your mum come from?
Second Wolf: Alaska.
First Wolf: Don't bother, I'll ask her myself.

What do you call a chicken in the jungle?
An eggs-plorer.

Teacher: Which family does the hippopotamus belong to?
Pupil: Don't ask me – nobody on our street owns one.

What do you call a deer with no eyes?
I've no eye-deer . . .

Teacher: Name three types of bird which can't fly.
Pupil: An ostrich, a penguin and a dead vulture.

What's the difference between an African elephant and an Indian elephant?
About seventy thousand miles.

How do you know when there's a
hippopotamus hiding under your bed?
*You wake up with your nose pressed
against the ceiling.*

What do you call a pig with no clothes
on?
Streaky bacon.

Why did the elephant jump on top of the
house?
Because he wanted a flat.

Where should you send a short-sighted
kangaroo?
To the hop-tician.

▲▼▲▼▲▼▲▼▲▼▲▼▲▼▲▼▲▼▲▼▲▼▲▼

Why did the two rhinos crash into each other?
They forgot to sound their horns.

What is a monkey's favourite ballet?
The Nutcracker.

What kind of bird lays electric eggs?
A battery hen.

What do you call a two-metre-high gorilla with a banana in each ear?
Anything you like – it can't hear you.

What's the safest way to own a wild animal?
Buy a tame one and then annoy it.

What part of a crocodile weighs the most?
Its scales.

What do you give a constipated sparrow?
Chirrup of figs.

How do fleas travel from one part of the jungle to another?
They itch-hike.

What's the difference between a buffalo and a bison?
You can't wash your hands in a buffalo.

What's the best cure for snakebites?
Stop biting snakes.

Why did the elephant sit on the tennis ball?
Because he wanted to play squash.

What do you call a snake with a Meccano set?
A boa constructor.

What did one jackal say to the other jackal?
'I've got a bone to pick with you.'

What do you call an elephant that keeps muttering to itself?
A mumbo-jumbo.

▲▽▲▽▲▽▲▽▲▽▲▽▲▽▲▽▲▽▲▽▲▽▲▽▲▽

Why did the crocodile buy a new suit?
He wanted to be a snappy dresser.

Quentin Quiver: Ouch! I've been bitten
by a mosquito!
Guide: So put some cream on it . . .
Quentin Quiver: Don't be silly, it'll have
flown away by now!

Which animal is always banned from
competitions?
The cheetah.

What's the difference between an antelope and Quentin Quiver?
One is a nervous, jumpy creature with not many brains . . . and the other's a wild animal.

HOW DO I KNOW OWLS ARE AS WISE AS YOU SAY?

WELL, FOR ONE THING I'M NOT STANDING THERE ASKING STUPID QUESTIONS WHEN THERE'S A TIGER BEHIND ME!

Why did the monkey tie banana skins to his feet?
He wanted a pair of slippers.

HELP! IT SEEMS LIKE I'VE BEEN TRYING TO GIVE MAD MONKEYS THE SLIP FOR THIS WHOLE CHAPTER!

SLIDE!!

NEVER MIND THE BANANAS... THERE'S A WHOLE NEW BUNCH OF JOKES STARTING ON THE NEXT PAGE!

Chapter Three

WHAT'S BLACK AND WHITE AND RED ALL OVER?

What should you give an orang-utan on his birthday?
A big round of ape-plause.

Where do you take sick insects?
To waspital.

Which animal is best at cricket?
The bat.

STOP, QUENTIN—
DON'T YOU WANT
TO STUDY
VAMPIRE
BATS?

IF I DO
I'M BOUND
TO END UP
OUT FOR
THE
COUNT!

Why couldn't the butterfly go to the dance?
Because it was a moth ball.

When's the best time to buy a budgie?
When they're going cheep.

Why do swallows fly south in winter?
Because it's too far to walk.

Where do eagles meet for coffee?
In a nest-café.

Why did the crocodile bite his own tail?
He was trying to make both ends meet.

What do you get when you cross a lion
with a lemon?
A sourpuss.

Do lions ever have fleas?
No, just baby lions.

Why did the caterpillar make a New
Year's Resolution?
It wanted to turn over a new leaf.

What swings around the jungle and
tastes like Christmas cake?
Tarzipan.

Where do very old alligators sleep?
In croc-ing chairs.

What's white and woolly and has really
sharp teeth?
A wolf in sheep's clothing.

What do rhinos have that no other animal has?
Baby rhinos.

When do rhinos have twelve legs?
When there are three of them.

Why are elephants so wrinkly?
Because they're really hard to iron.

How do you start a bear race?
'Ready, Teddy, Go!'

Why was the firefly sent home from school?
He'd forgotten to wear his blazer.

First monkey: Where do fleas go in winter?
Second monkey: Search me!

Teacher: Spell 'Elephant'.
Pupil: E-L-E-P-H-A-N
Teacher: But what's at the end of it?
Pupil: A little grey tail.

What did the lion say to his barber?
'You're my mane man.'

Which snake is best at sums?
The adder.

What's green and slimy and goes dot dot
dot dash dash dash?
A Morse toad.

What is the kangaroo's favourite year?
Leap Year.

What do porcupines like to find in their lunchboxes?
Prickled onions.

Where do you send a sick bird?
For tweetment.

How do otters travel along the riverbank?
In their otter-mobiles.

Why did the wolf sneak up behind the sheep and shout 'Hey, you!'?
He wanted to make a ewe turn.

What do you get if you cross an owl with a skunk?
A bird that stinks but doesn't give a hoot.

What do you get if you cross Lassie with a geranium?
A collie flower.

What do you get if you cross Lassie with a vampire bat?
A blood-hound.

What do you get if you cross an elk with an eclair?
A chocolate moose.

What do you call two elephants having a chat?
A heavy discussion.

'Doctor, Doctor, I keep thinking I'm a chameleon.'
'Nonsense – you're just a little off colour.'

WHAT KIND OF A CHAMELEON ARE YOU – YOU NEVER CHANGE COLOUR!

THAT'S 'COS YOU ALWAYS MAKE ME SEE RED!!

'Doctor, Doctor, I keep thinking I'm a goat.'
'How long have you felt like this?'
'Ever since I was a kid.'

'Doctor, Doctor, I keep thinking I'm a crocodile.'
'Oh, snap out of it.'

What's green and scaly and lives under a rock on the Yellow Brick Road?
The Lizard of Oz.

What do vampire bats do before taking off?
They always look in their wing mirrors.

What do you get if you cross a duck with Santa?
A Christmas quacker.

'Doctor, Doctor, I keep thinking I'm a horse.'
'I can cure you – but it's going to be expensive!'
'No problem – last Saturday I won the Grand National.'

What was the python's favourite party game?
Swallow my leader.

Chapter Four

WHAT TIME IS IT WHEN THE HIPPO SITS ON THE FENCE?

TIME YOU REALISED THAT THERE AREN'T ANY FENCES IN THE JUNGLE...

ARRGH! THAT'S NO REASON TO SIT ON ME INSTEAD!

'Doctor, Doctor, I think I'm turning into a frog.'
'Well, do it in the croakroom.'

Did you hear about the short-sighted porcupine?
It fell in love with a cactus.

What goes 'woof woof tock'?
A watch dog.

What do you get if you pour boiling water down a rabbit hole?
Hot cross bunnies.

Why did the kangaroo go into the Chinese restaurant?
To order some Hop Suey.

What do you call a buffalo in a revolving door?
Stuck!

What do you get if you cross a cow, a sheep and a goat?
The Milky Baa Kid.

What do you get if you cross a gorilla, a cow and a python?
A banana milksnake.

What do you get if you cross a motorway with a giant tortoise?
Run over.

Did you hear about the lion who swallowed a goose?
He felt a little down in the mouth.

What do you call an elephant on a diving board?
A big dipper.

What do you get if you cross a hedgehog with a fir tree?
A porcu-pine.

What do centipedes eat for breakfast?
Scrambled legs.

Why are giraffes so cheap to feed?
Because even a little goes a long way.

What's got horns, udders and cuts grass?
A lawnmooer.

What do you get if you cross a tiger with a footballer?
A very nervous referee.

What do you call a camel with three humps?
Humphrey.

What is snakeskin used for?
To stop the snake's insides from falling out.

What do you call a penguin in the jungle?
Lost.

What's the most breathless animal in the jungle?
The pant-her.

LIONS, PANTHERS, LEOPARDS... IF I LET ANY OF THEM CATCH ME IT'LL BE A REAL "CAT-ASTROPHE!"

'Doctor, Doctor, my mum thinks she's a parrot.'
'Well why can't she come and see me herself?'
'We don't like letting her out of the cage.'

What's sweet and juicy, but very painful to eat?
A porcu-pineapple.

Why are four-legged animals bad dancers?
Because they have two left feet.

'Doctor, Doctor, I keep thinking I'm a chicken.'
'You'd better go to hospital for a few days.'
'I can't – my family needs the eggs.'

What's the name of the world's worst liontamer?
Claude Bottom.

WHAT DID THE LION SAY TO THE LION TAMER?

YOU'RE GETTIN UNDER MY SKIN!

'Doctor, Doctor, I keep thinking I'm an anteater. Can you help me?'
'Certainly – stick out your tongue.'
'OK – do you want the whole lot or just the first two metres?'

WHO'S THE SNOBBIEST ANIMAL IN THE JUNGLE?

THE ANTEATER – HE LOOKS DOWN HIS NOSE AT EVERYONE!

What do you get if you cross a bison with a platypus?
A buffalo bill.

'Doctor, Doctor, everywhere I look I see kangaroos.'
'Don't worry – it's just a hop-tical illusion.'

What is the least intelligent creature in the jungle?
Quentin Quiver – if he had any intelligence he wouldn't have come into the jungle in the first place.

Why is the aardvark the least dangerous animal in the jungle?
Because aardvark never killed anyone.

Did you hear the story about the elephant sandwich?
It's a bit hard to swallow.

Why are leopards no good at Hide and Seek?
Because they are always spotted.

Which is stronger, a turtle or an elephant?
The turtle because it carries its entire house on its back. The elephant only has to carry a trunk.

I CAN'T BELIEVE I'M BEING CHASED BY A TURTLE!!

SINCE HE STARTED HANGING AROUND WITH ELEPHANTS HE'S REALLY COME OUT OF HIS SHELL!

What did the big cobra say to the little cobra?
'You're the spitting image of your father.'

How did the firefly feel when its tail fell off?
It was de-lighted.

'Did you know that it takes over a dozen sheep to make a single sweater?'
'Really? I didn't even know they could knit.'

Did you hear about the hippo who sat on a biscuit?
Yes – it's a pretty crumby joke.

What is the kangaroo's favourite shampoo?
Wash and pogo.

First Bat: Fancy going out for a bite?
Second Bat: No, I think I'll just hang around.

LEAVE ME ALONE! I KEEP TELLING YOU I'M NOT YOUR COUSIN!

BUT YOU MUST BE BATS TO STAY IN A BOOK LIKE THIS ONE!

Why is the jungle a happier place when all the gnus go on holiday?
Because no gnus is good gnus.

What do fireflies do first thing in the morning?
Rise and shine.

What's got black and white stripes and can see just as well from both ends?
A zebra with its eyes shut.

HERE IT IS IN BLACK AND WHITE, QUENTIN... WE WANT YOU OUT OF HERE!

OUCH! I'M GETTING HASSLED BY A WHOLE RANGE OF ANIMALS FROM 'A' TO 'ZEBRA'!

WHACK!

QUENTIN WON'T GET A KICK OUT OF THE JOKES IN THE NEXT CHAPTER EITHER...

Chapter Five

KNOCK, KNOCK! WHO'S THERE? ANT ANT WHO?

Who is the mosquito's favourite singer?
Sting.

What did one bee say to the other bee?
'Swarm in here, isn't it?'

What was the frog's favourite drink?
Croak-a-cola.

What says: 'Now you see me, now you don't, now you see me, now you don't.'?
A panda on a zebra crossing.

▲▼▲▼▲▼▲▼▲▼▲▼▲▼▲▼▲▼▲▼▲▼▲▼▲▼

How do you know when your
chameleon's sick?
It doesn't turn a funny colour.

What's grey, has a big horn, and drinks
too much?
A wine-oceros.

What do you call an ant with a tube of
glue?
A stick insect.

HELP! I'M STUCK!!

WHO SAYS QUENTIN ISN'T ENJOYING THE REALLY BEASTLY JOKE BOOK!

YEAH- HE CAN'T SEEM TO TEAR HIMSELF AWAY!

Why are rabbits good at maths?
Because they multiply very quickly.

What do skunks use to keep their fur
clean?
Sham-poo.

What are big, white and furry and have holes in the middle?
Polo bears.

What did the cheetah do when the elephant started chasing him?
About sixty-five miles per hour.

EVERYONE KNOWS CHEETAHS RUN REALLY FAST BUT ISN'T THERE ALSO A FACT ABOUT ELEPHANTS' MEMORIES?

YES— BUT I FORGET WHAT IT IS!

Why must you always drive slowly in the jungle?
Because you never know when you're going to come across a zebra crossing.

What's the worse name you can give your pet zebra?
Spot.

What do you get if you cross an alligator
with a judge?
*The tooth, the whole tooth and nothing
but the tooth.*

Which shampoo turns your hair pink?
Wash and flamingo.

'Waiter – there's a mosquito in my soup.'
'Don't worry, sir – mosquitoes have very
small appetites.'

What do you sing to a skunk on his
birthday?
'For He's A Jolly Good Smeller.'

Why is Quentin Quiver afraid of wild animals?
Because he suffers from claws-trophobia.

What's big, grey and has sixteen wheels?
An elephant on roller skates.

Why are camels so bad-tempered?
Because they've always got the hump.

Did you hear about the giraffe who
swallowed a bell?
The vicar threatened to wring his neck.

Quentin Quiver: How much is that
parrot?
Pet Shop Owner: Twenty pounds.
Quentin Quiver: All right – send me the
bill.
Pet Shop Owner: Forget it – it's the whole
bird or nothing.

Why did the pig fail his driving test?
He was a road hog.

Why was the woodworm depressed?
Because his life was always boring.

Guide: Do you like eating spiders?
Quentin Quiver: Of course not!
Guide: That's a shame – because one just crawled into your sandwich.

Why shouldn't you be afraid of snakes?
Because they're all perfectly armless.

Why do kangaroos hate rainy days?
Because their youngsters want to play indoors.

Did you hear about the skunk who robbed a bank?
The police were on his scent in no time.

Why did the mole give up digging?
He was tired of the hole business.

First snake: Quick – are we poisonous?
Second snake: No – why do you ask?
First snake: I've just bitten my tongue.

Why was the teenage goat angry with his
parents?
He didn't like being treated like a kid.

Did you hear about the bull that went
into a china shop?
He had a smashing time.

Why did the snake swallow the firefly?
He fancied a light snack.

How does a monkey make toast?
He puts it under a gorilla.

HELP! YOU CAN'T SPREAD ME ON YOUR BREAD – I'M NOT MARMALADE!

NO.. BUT YOU'RE CERTAINLY IN A JAM.

▲▽▲▽▲▽▲▽▲▽▲▽▲▽▲▽▲▽▲▽▲▽▲▽▲▽

What do you call an elephant with no feelings?
Numbo.

What do you call an elephant with no teeth?
Gumbo.

WAITING ROOM

WHAT'S THE FIRST THING YOU'RE GOING TO EAT WHEN THE DENTIST IS FINISHED WITH YOU?

THE DENTIST.

Why was the pony coughing?
Because he was a little horse.

Want to buy a joke about two elks?
No, it's two deer.

What's two metres long and looks after sheep?
Little Boa Peep.

Why did no-one guess the stick insect
was bald?
He was wearing a very convincing twig.

Did you hear about the ostrich who
swallowed a bunch of keys?
He cured himself of lockjaw.

Chapter Six

WHAT DO YOU GET IF YOU CROSS A RHINO WITH A HYENA?

Where in the jungle do rhinos sleep?
Anywhere they jolly well like.

What's hairy, eats bananas and isn't very clever?
A chumpanzee.

Why are giraffes brave?
Because they believe in sticking their necks out.

What's green and hairy and goes up and down?
A gooseberry in a kangaroo's pocket.

What should you give a seasick hippo?
Lots and lots of room.

What do you call an angry blackbird?
Raven mad.

What do you get if you cross a skunk with a chicken?
A really fowl smell.

Why did the snake buy an apple for the teacher?
Because it was a bit of a crawler.

How do you know which end of a worm is its head?
Tickle it and see which end smiles.

'Doctor, Doctor, I keep thinking I'm a dog.'
'I'd better examine you – lie down on the couch.'
'I can't – I'm not allowed up on the furniture.'

Police chief: You've still got that chimpanzee you found? I thought I told you to take it to the zoo?
Constable: I did take it to the zoo . . .
and tonight I'm taking it to the pictures.

WHY DID THE CHIMPANZEE BRING A BANANA SKIN TO THE CINEMA?

SO HE COULD SLIP IN WHEN THE MANAGER WASN'T LOOKING!

What does the mummy alligator sing to her children?
'Croc-a-bye baby.'

Why did the alligator buy a mobile phone?
He wanted to croco-dial.

Vet: What's your dog's name?
Owner: I don't know – he won't tell us.

Why did the gorilla put suntan-oil on his
banana?
He wanted to stop it peeling.

What time do ducks get up?
At the quack of dawn.

How do hens dance?
Chick to chick.

Why did the polar bears invite the
kangaroo to visit?
*Because it was cold and they needed a
jumper.*

What do you get if you cross a cow with an octopus?
I don't know – but at least it can milk itself.

Why did the big group of elephants paint themselves bright pink?
They wanted to be seen and not herd.

What did the bison say when it joined
the police force?
'Buffalo, allo allo.'

What's big and grey and always falling
over?
A trip-opotamus.

Elephant: See? I told you I could do a
headstand really easily.
Quentin Quiver: Yes, but that's because
it's *my* head you're standing on.

What newspaper do skunks read?
Phews of the World.

Quentin Quiver: Ouch! A mosquito's bitten me just under my nose!
Guide: That will help you to keep a stiff upper lip.

I hear you've got a good joke about the lion?
Yes – it'll really make you roar.

What's big and grey and never gets wet?
An umbrellaphant.

Heard the joke about the eagle?
Well, never mind – it would probably just go over your head.

Why are giraffes so snooty?
Because they look down on everyone.

What's black and white and furry and
comes down the chimney?
Panda Claus.

Have you heard the joke about the polar
bear?
Yes, but it left me cold.

What do fireflies sing at football matches?
'Here we glow, here we glow, here we glow . . .'

Why did the elephant leave the circus?
He was tired of working for peanuts.

What do you get if you cross a hyena with a parrot?
An animal that laughs at its own jokes.

HAVE YOU HEARD THE ONE ABOUT THE TALKING PARROT?

YES - BUT I'M NOT ALLOWED TO REPEAT IT!

Where do you find giant snails?
On the end of giants' fingers.

'Doctor, Doctor, I keep thinking I'm a mosquito.'
'Well, take these tablets and if they don't work, give me a buzz.'

What's big and grey and has a big hole
in the back of its trousers?
A hippo-botty-mus.

Why didn't the rhino get lost in the
mist?
Because he had a foghorn.

What was the mouse's favourite party
game?
Hide and Squeak.

What's big and grey and always out of
bed by six a.m.?
An early-phant.

Who was the most important python in Rome?
Julius Squeezer.

What do you get if you cross a sheepdog with a bowl of jelly?
The collie wobbles.

Why do baby kangaroos always need money?
Because they are often out of pocket.

Chapter Seven

'DOCTOR, DOCTOR, CAN YOU CURE ME OF MY FEAR OF SNAKES?'

'YES – IN FACT I PROMISE YOU'LL NEVER WORRY ABOUT SNAKES AGAIN.'

'HOW CAN YOU BE SURE ABOUT THAT?'

BECAUSE YOU'LL BE TOO BUSY WORRYING ABOUT MY PET LION CATCHING YOU!!

EEK! I'D BE 'LION' IF I SAID I WASN'T TERRIFIED!!

What do ghostly pandas eat?
*Bam*BOO!

BOO!

AIEEE! LOOKS LIKE THIS CHAPTER'S GOING TO BE FULL OF MORE PANDA-MONIUM!

Who's the best timekeeper in the jungle?
The clock-odile.

'Doctor, Doctor, I keep thinking I'm a chameleon.'
'Don't worry – the change should do you good.'

What did the baby ostrich say when it saw its mum sitting on an orange?
'Look what marmalade!'

What do birds say on Halloween?
'Trick or Tweet.'

Why did the tiger try and sell his roller skates?
Because the other animals were pushing him around.

WHY DID THE TIGER GET A TICKET?

OH!

HE PARKED HIS ROLLER SKATES ON A DOUBLE YELLOW LION..

What runs through the jungle at Christmas shouting 'Ho ho ho'?
A Santa-lope.

Did you hear about the miser who kept feeding pound coins to his cat?
He wanted to have some money in the kitty.

Quentin Quiver: I want to complain – your dog's been chasing me on my bike!
Owner: Don't be silly – my dog can't even ride a bike!

Quentin Quiver: Got any little kittens
going cheap?
Petshop owner: No – all of ours go
'Miaow'.

What's the crocodile's favourite
cardgame?
Snap!

What's big and grey and flies all over the jungle?
An ele-copter.

What do you get when you cross a sheep and a porcupine?
Something that can knit its own sweaters.

What do you get when you cross an elephant and a budgie?
A very messy cage.

What changes colour every time it tells a joke?
A stand-up chameleon.

Why are hens rude?
Because they're always using fowl language.

Did you hear about the leopard who fell in the washing-machine?
He came out spotless.

Why should Quentin Quiver be grateful if a mosquito stings him?
It's the only way to make him smart.

What do you get if you dip a hyena in beer?
A barrel of laughs.

Why did the snake go on holiday?
He wanted to relax and unwind.

What should you do if a rhinoceros steps
on your foot?
Limp.

Where do chameleons spend most of
their time at school?
In the changing rooms.

IT TAKES A LONG TIME TO LEARN TO CHANGE COLOUR...

...BUT QUENTIN'S GOING TO BE BLACK AND BLUE BY THE TIME WE FINISH WITH HIM!

Why do giraffes find it difficult to
apologize?
*It takes them a long time to swallow their
pride.*

What do sleepy vultures pick on?
Lazy bones.

What do you get if you cross a budgie
with a porcupine?
Shredded tweet.

What do you call a gorilla in a prison
uniform?
A Kongvict.

Why did the kangaroo go to the disco?
He heard they were looking for bouncers.

Which bird spends most of its time underground?
A mynah bird.

Is it safe to chase a wild rhino with a club?
Only if the club has more than two hundred members.

First Lion: What are you doing in this part of the jungle?
Second Lion: I'm hunting for antelope.
First Lion: But there are no antelope around here.
Second Lion: If there were, I wouldn't have to hunt for them, would I?

Quentin Quiver: This flea-powder you sold me is useless!

Shopkeeper: How do you mean, useless?

Quentin Quiver: The fleas won't stay still long enough for me to put the powder on them.

'Waiter – there's a stick insect in my soup.'

'You'll have to call the branch manager.'

What's the difference between an angry rabbit and a fake ten-pound note?

One's a mad bunny and the other's bad money.

What's big and greasy and covered with salt?

A chippopotamus.

What do you get if you cross a vampire
bat with a sausage?
A fangfurter.

SHOULDN'T A VAMPIRE
BAT BE IN 'THE HAUNTED
JOKE BOOK' INSTEAD OF
THIS
ONE?

I KNOW, BUT
I'M JUST PAYING
A FLYING
VISIT!

Quentin Quiver: Doctor, Doctor, a
mosquito bit me on the ankle.
Doctor: Didn't you put anything on it?
Quentin Quiver: No – he liked the taste
just as it was.

Quentin Quiver: Uh oh – there's a big
black cat following us!
Guide: That's very lucky!
Quentin Quiver: Not when it's a panther.

Why did the spider complain
to the waiter?
Because there wasn't *a fly in his soup.*

Why bird is always out of breath?
The puffin.

What did the tiger say when it saw
Quentin Quiver in his sleeping-bag?
'Look – breakfast in bed.'

What changes colour every two seconds?
A chameleon with hiccups.

Which gorilla had six wives?
King Henry the Ape.

Chapter Eight

WHAT'S THE DIFFERENCE BETWEEN A CROCODILE AND AN ALLIGATOR?

THE CROCODILE WANTS QUENTIN FOR DINNER...

...WHILE THE ALLIGATOR FANCIES HIM FOR LUNCH!

EITHER WAY, I'VE BITTEN OFF MORE THAN I CAN CHEW...

Why do storks stand on one leg?
Because if they lifted the other one they'd fall on their bottoms.

What hops around the Outback all day shouting 'Knickers!'?
A kanga-rude.

WHAT DOES QUENTIN QUIVER DO WHEN A KANGAROO TRIES TO STEAL HIS UNDIES?

HE PULLS UNTIL HE PUFFS AND PANTS...

DON'T LET GO, MUM— I NEED NEW CURTAINS FOR MY ROOM!!

NO WAY! IF I LET GO IT WILL BE CURTAINS FOR ME!!

What's big, grey, has a trunk and goes 'Woof woof'?
An elephant doing impressions.

What did one python say to the other python?
'I've got a crush on you.'

What do you get if you cross a tiger with a cow?
An animal that eats anyone who tries to milk it.

What do you get if you cross a biscuit with an elephant?
Crumbs.

What do you get when you cross an elephant with a kangaroo?
Something that causes an earthquake every time it hops.

How do we know owls are smarter than chickens?
Have you ever heard of Kentucky Fried Owl?

Did you hear about the cobra who hid inside a tuba?
It was a lowdown snake in the brass.

Why are turkeys bad mannered?
Because they always gobble their dinners.

MERRY CHRISTMAS, MR TURKEY...

YES...BUT GUESS WHICH ONE OF US IS ABOUT TO GET STUFFED!

Guide: Calm down, Quentin Quiver, that snake you saw is just a baby.
Quentin: How do you know it's a baby?
Guide: Because it's got a rattle.

Why are small trees like baby elephants?
They've both only got little trunks.

What's black and white and never wants to grow up?
Peter Panda.

What's got very sharp teeth and lives at the end of the rainbow?
A croc of gold.

Did you hear about the snake who swallowed a frog?
The vet says he could croak at any minute.

HEY! COME BACK HERE AND DON'T MAKE ME SHOUT AT YOU!!

DON'T WORRY — I'M DOING MY BEST TO MAKE SURE YOU DON'T GET A FROG IN YOUR THROAT!

Did you hear about the hen who was running a temperature?
She kept laying hard-boiled eggs.

Which cows live at the North Pole?
Eskimoos.

What goes 'Clomp, clomp, squish, clomp, clomp, squish'?
An elephant with a wet shoe.

What do you get when you cross a
centipede with a parrot?
A walkie-talkie.

What do giant snails use to decorate
their shells?
Snail varnish.

What do you call a pig in a laundrette?
Hogwash.

What do you call a tiger in the chemist's
shop?
Puss in Boots.

What sound do porcupines make when
they are kissing?
'OUCH!

"Doctor, Doctor, my brother thinks he's a firefly.'

'Are you sure you'll be able to afford the treatment?'

'Oh yes – we've already saved a fortune on lighting bills.'

Did you hear about the ostrich who swallowed a guitar?

Yes – now he makes music whenever he's plucked.

What do you get if you cross a watch with a hen?

An alarm cluck.

What's red and yellow and green and gold, purple and orange and blue?
A chameleon walking across a patchwork quilt.

Why are kangaroos good parents?
Because they always have bouncing babies.

Quentin Quiver: Quick! Have gooseberries got legs?
Guide: No.
Quentin Quiver: Oh no, I've swallowed a caterpillar!

Why are centipedes no good at football?
It takes them ninety minutes to change into their boots.

Why did the mice go to First Aid
classes?
To learn mouse-to-mouse resuscitation.

What do you get if you cross a kangaroo
with a zebra?
A striped jumper with a big pocket.

How should you treat a bear with a sore
head?
With the greatest respect.

How do you stop a rhino from charging?
Hide his battery.

Did you hear about the cat who swallowed
a ball of wool?
She had mittens.

What do you get if you cross a giraffe
with a rooster?
*An animal that can wake you up even
when you're on the 14th floor.*

Did you hear about the chicken who fell
in a cement-mixer?
She became a bricklayer.

What do rhinos have for their breakfast?
Hornflakes.

Where did the skunk play in the jungle
football team?
Scent-er forward.

'Doctor, Doctor, my sister thinks she's a
grizzly bear.'
'How soon can you bring her to the
surgery?'
*'Next spring, when she comes out of
hibernation.'*

What do grizzlies bring on their holidays?
Just the bear necessities.

RELAX, QUENTIN- YOU'VE MADE IT TO THE END OF THE BOOK... NOW WE ANIMALS HAVE FOUND SOMEWHERE DARK AND HIDDEN FOR YOU WHERE NO OTHER BEAST CAN GET YOU!
REALLY? SOUNDS GOOD- IS IT JUST BEYOND THAT LAST JOKE?

AND
FINALLY . . .

WHY DID QUENTIN QUIVER CROSS THE JUNGLE IN THE OTHER DIRECTION?

▲▼▲▼▲▼▲▼▲▼▲▼▲▼▲▼▲▼▲▼▲▼▲▼▲▼▲▼▲▼▲▼▲▼▲▼

▲▼▲▼▲▼▲▼▲▼▲▼▲▼▲▼▲▼▲▼▲▼▲▼▲▼▲▼